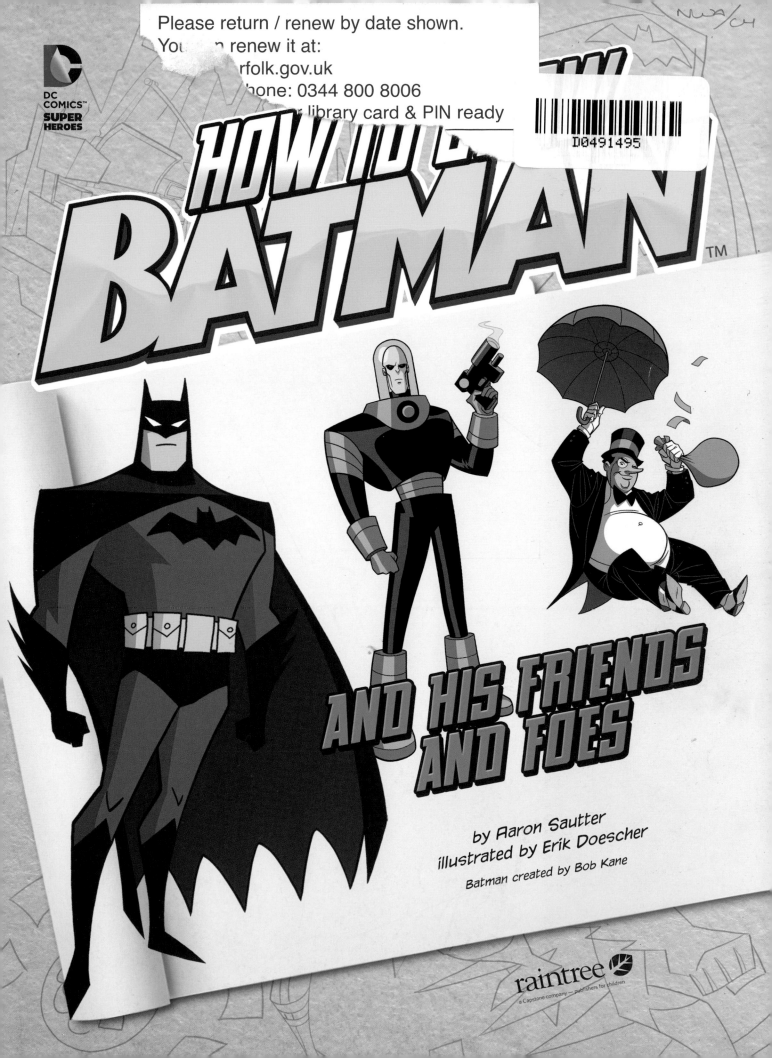

DC COMICS™ SUPER HEROES

HOW TO DRAW BATMAN™

AND HIS FRIENDS AND FOES

by Aaron Sautter

illustrated by Erik Doescher

Batman created by Bob Kane

raintree
a Capstone company — publishers for children

Raintree is an imprint of Capstone Global Library Limited, a company incorporated in England and Wales having its registered office at 7 Pilgrim Street, London, EC4V 6LB – Registered company number: 6695582

www.raintree.co.uk
myorders@raintree.co.uk

STAR33521

Credits

Designer: Ted Williams
Art Director: Nathan Gassman
Production Specialist: Kathy McColley

ISBN 978 1 406 29192 6
18 17 16 15 14
10 9 8 7 6 5 4 3 2 1

British Library Cataloguing in Publication Data

A full catalogue record for this book is available from the British Library.

Design Elements

Capstone Studio: Karon Dubke
Shutterstock: Artishok, Bennyartist, Eliks, gst, Mazzzur, Roobcio

Every effort has been made to contact copyright holders of material reproduced in this book. Any omissions will be rectified in subsequent printings if notice is given to the publisher.

Printed and bound in China.

DRAWING PROJECTS

LET'S DRAW THE DARK KNIGHT!

He's been called the World's Greatest Detective, the Caped Crusader and the Dark Knight. But whatever people choose to call him — Batman is a criminal's worst nightmare.

As a young boy, Bruce Wayne lost his parents, Thomas and Martha, during a robbery in a dark alley. Bruce was deeply affected by his parents' death. He swore an oath that he would do whatever it took to rid Gotham City of criminals and crime. To achieve his goal, Bruce studied criminology to learn detective skills. He also trained hard to become an expert in martial arts. He even became a master of disguise and an expert escape artist.

Bruce's new skills were useful, but they weren't enough for him. He also wanted to strike fear into the hearts of criminals. Bruce chose to use his own fear of bats as his inspiration. He made a special suit that resembled a giant bat to hide his identity and to frighten hardened criminals. With his Batsuit and unmatched crime-fighting skills, Bruce became Batman: the Dark Knight.

Welcome to the world of Batman! On the following pages you'll learn to draw Batman, his friends and several of his most infamous enemies.

Imagine the streets of Gotham City and see what kind of amazing Batman drawings you can create!

WHAT YOU'LL NEED

You don't need superpowers to draw mighty heroes. But you'll need some basic tools. Gather the following stationery before starting your amazing art.

PAPER: You can get special drawing paper from art and craft shops. But any type of blank, unlined paper will be fine.

PENCILS: Drawings should be done in pencil first. Even professionals use them. If you make a mistake, it'll be easy to rub out and redraw. Keep plenty of these essential drawing tools on hand.

PENCIL SHARPENER: To make clean lines, you need to keep your pencils sharp. Get a good pencil sharpener. You'll use it a lot.

ERASERS: As you draw, you're bound to make mistakes. Erasers give artists the power to turn back time and rub out those mistakes. Get some high quality rubber or kneaded erasers. They'll last a lot longer than pencil erasers.

BLACK FELT-TIP PENS: When your drawing is ready, trace over the final lines with black felt-tip pen. The dark lines will help to make your characters stand out on the page.

COLOURED PENCILS AND PENS: Ready to finish your masterpiece? Bring your characters to life and give them some colour with coloured pencils or pens.

5

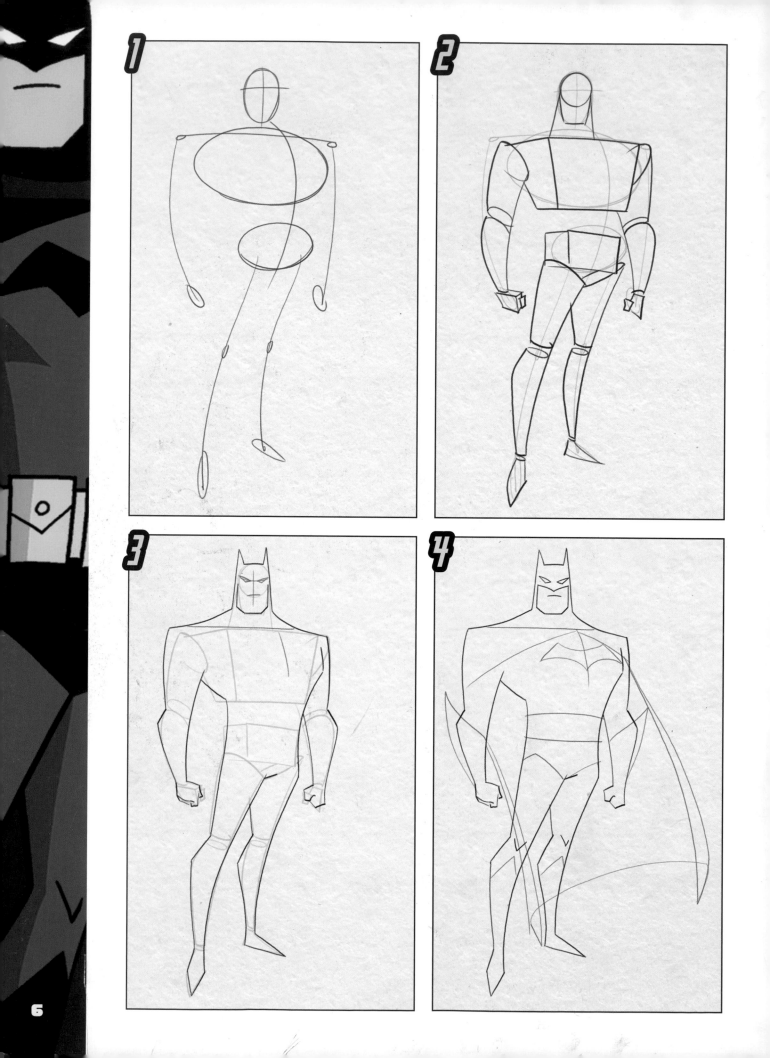

BATSUIT

Batman wouldn't be Batman without his Batsuit. The suit's main purpose is to hide Bruce Wayne's identity, while striking terror into the hearts of criminals. The suit also helps Batman to hide in the shadows as he prowls through the night. Batman's Utility Belt holds his many crime-fighting tools, including Batarangs, a grapnel, binoculars and remote controls for his vehicles.

BATCAVE

Sometimes the World's Greatest Detective needs a quiet place to think. When Batman needs answers, he goes to his secret Batcave. There, he uses the powerful Batcomputer to study clues and find the information he needs. The Batcave is also home to Batman's amazing vehicles and the workshop where he creates his incredible crime-fighting gadgets.

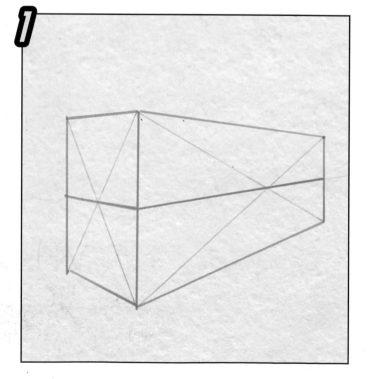

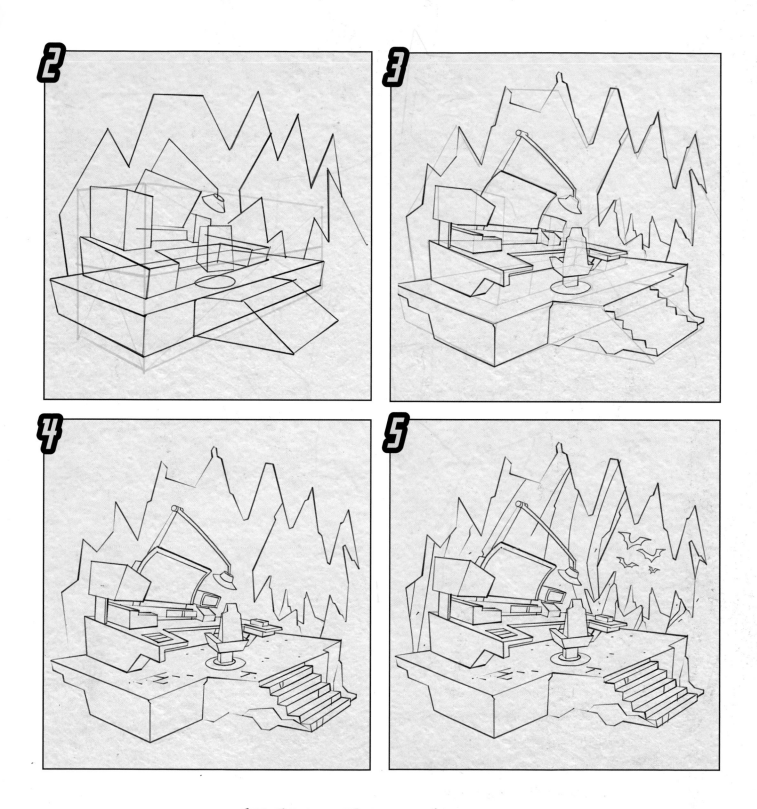

DRAWING IDEA
Next try drawing the Batmobile blasting out of the Batcave's secret entrance!

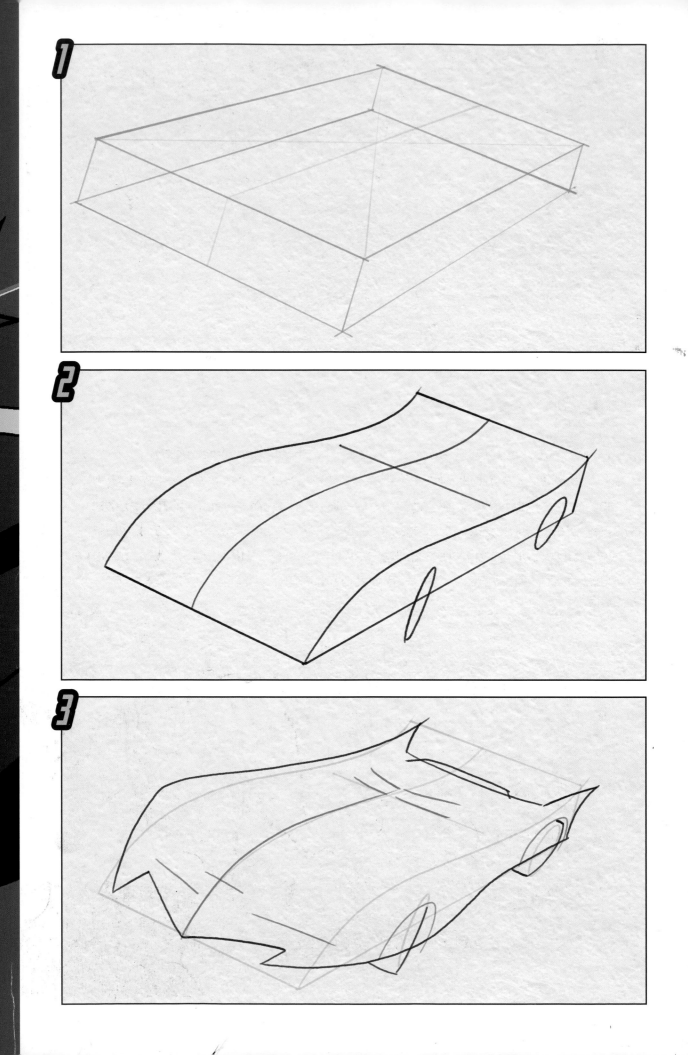

BATMOBILE

When Batman needs to be somewhere fast, he relies on the Batmobile to get him there. With its jet-powered engine, this speedy car helps Batman to get across Gotham City in a flash. Batman also uses the Batmobile to chase down villains in their getaway cars. This armoured car is equipped with grappling hooks and road spikes. It can also create slippery oil slicks to stop criminals from escaping.

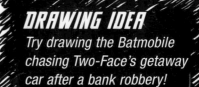

DRAWING IDEA
Try drawing the Batmobile chasing Two-Face's getaway car after a bank robbery!

FIGHTING CRIME

Criminals in Gotham City don't stand a chance with Batman around. He's always on the lookout for thugs trying to break the law. When a super-villain like Bane tries to rob a bank, the Dark Knight is on the case. Bane is very intelligent and has superhuman strength. But Batman's fighting skills and experience can stop the master criminal in his tracks!

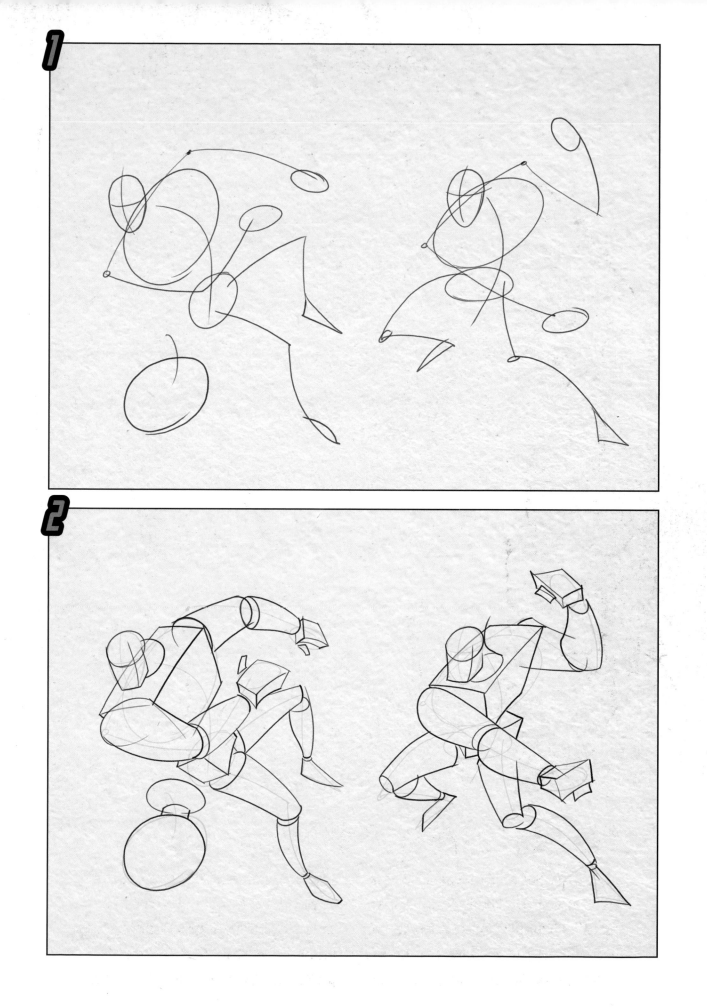

DRAWING IDEA
Try drawing Robin fighting next to Batman as they put a stop to the Riddler's plans!

ROBIN, THE BOY WONDER

Real Name: Tim Drake

Home Base: Gotham City

Occupation: student, crime fighter

Abilities: martial arts expert, investigation skills

Background: Tim Drake is quite brilliant for his age. Using his keen observation skills, Tim discovered the secret identities of both Batman and Nightwing. Nightwing once fought crime next to Batman as the first Robin. Nightwing then helped Tim to convince Batman that he needed a new partner. Tim now fights crime alongside Batman as the all new Robin, the Boy Wonder.

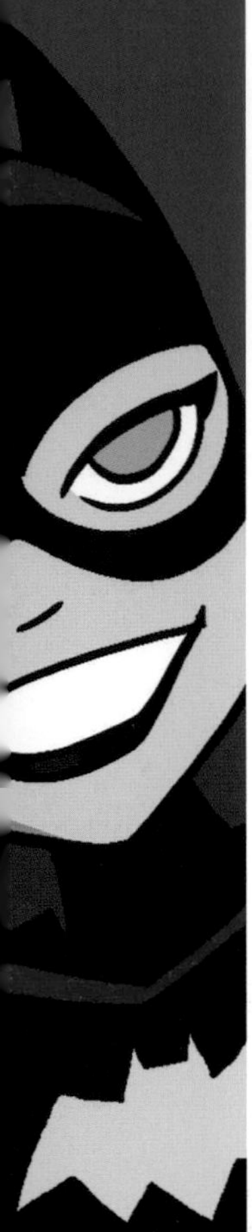

1

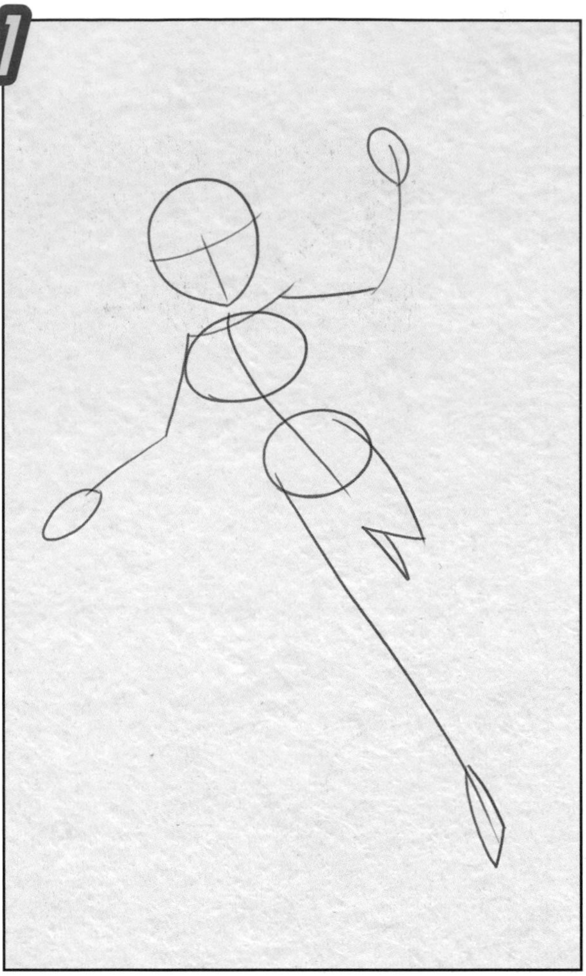

2

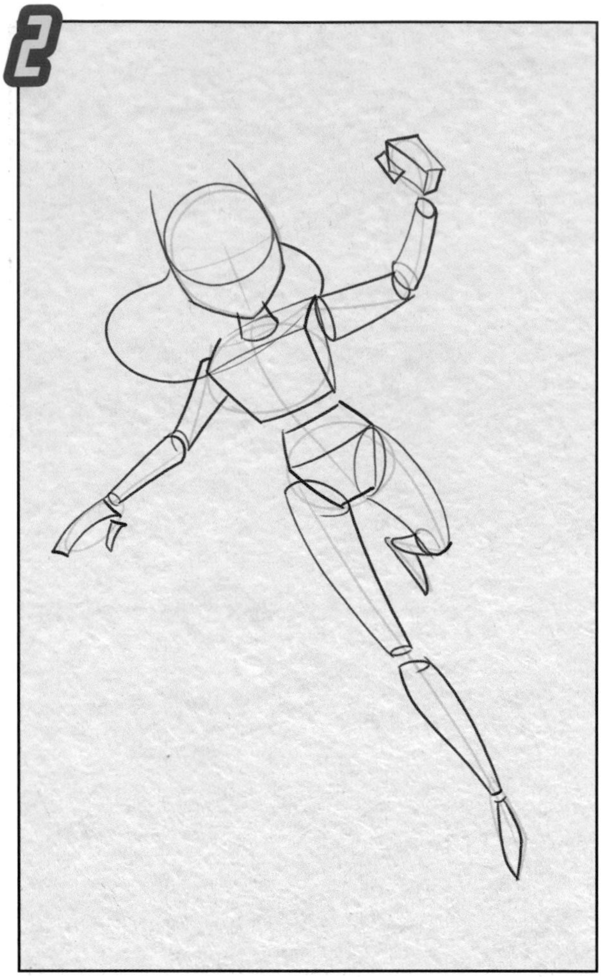

3

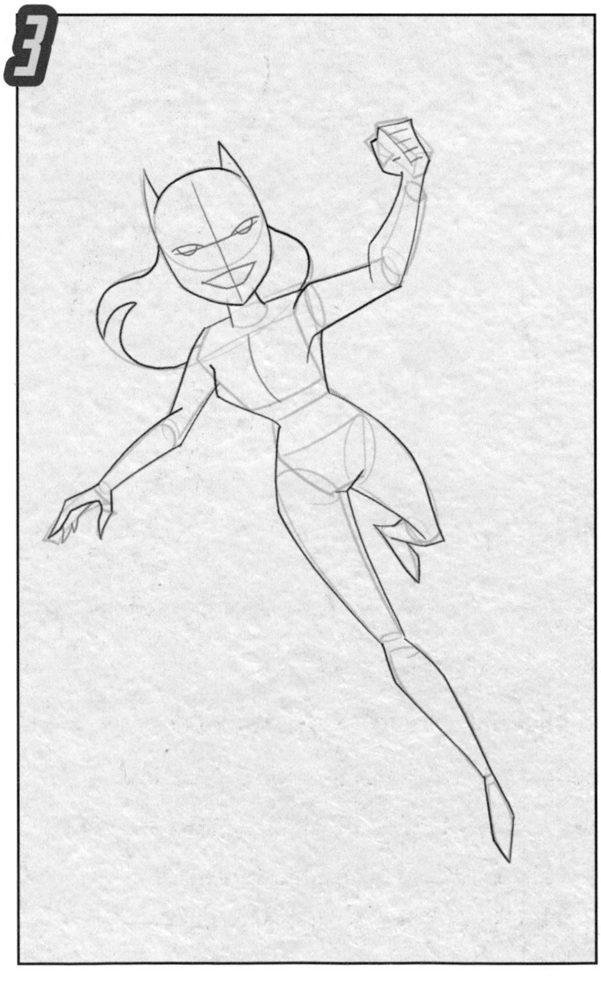

4

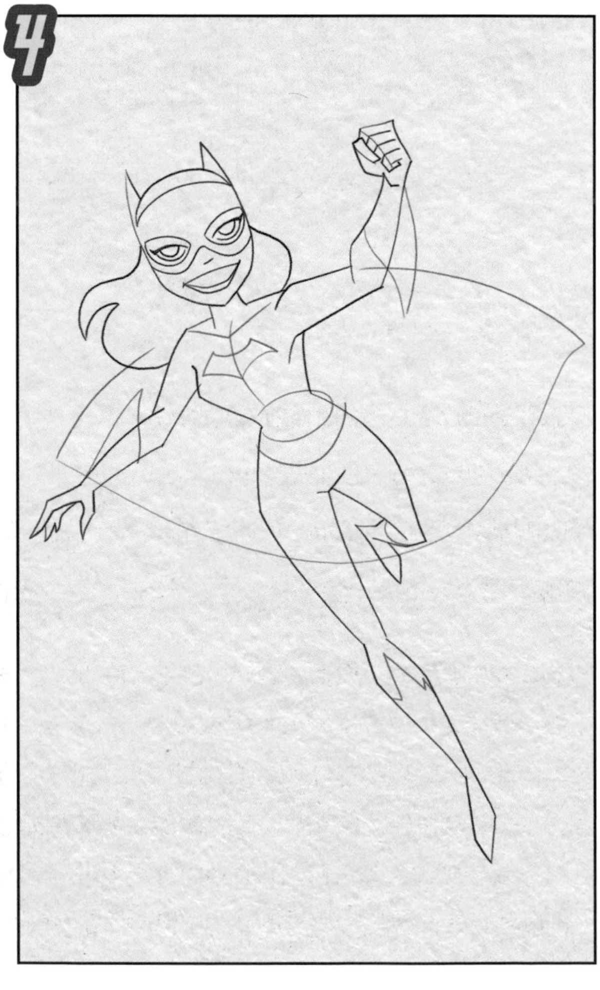

DRAWING IDEA
Try drawing Batgirl working with Robin to track down the Penguin and his thugs!

BATGIRL

Real Name: Barbara Gordon

Home Base: Gotham City

Occupation: college student, crime fighter

Abilities: gymnastics, martial arts skills

Background: Barbara Gordon takes after her father, Police Commissioner James Gordon. She is strong-willed and dedicated to wiping out crime from Gotham City. When Barbara's father was framed for a crime he didn't commit, she made her own bat-themed suit and attempted to break him out of jail. Since then Batgirl has become part of Batman's team, helping him to defend Gotham City from crime.

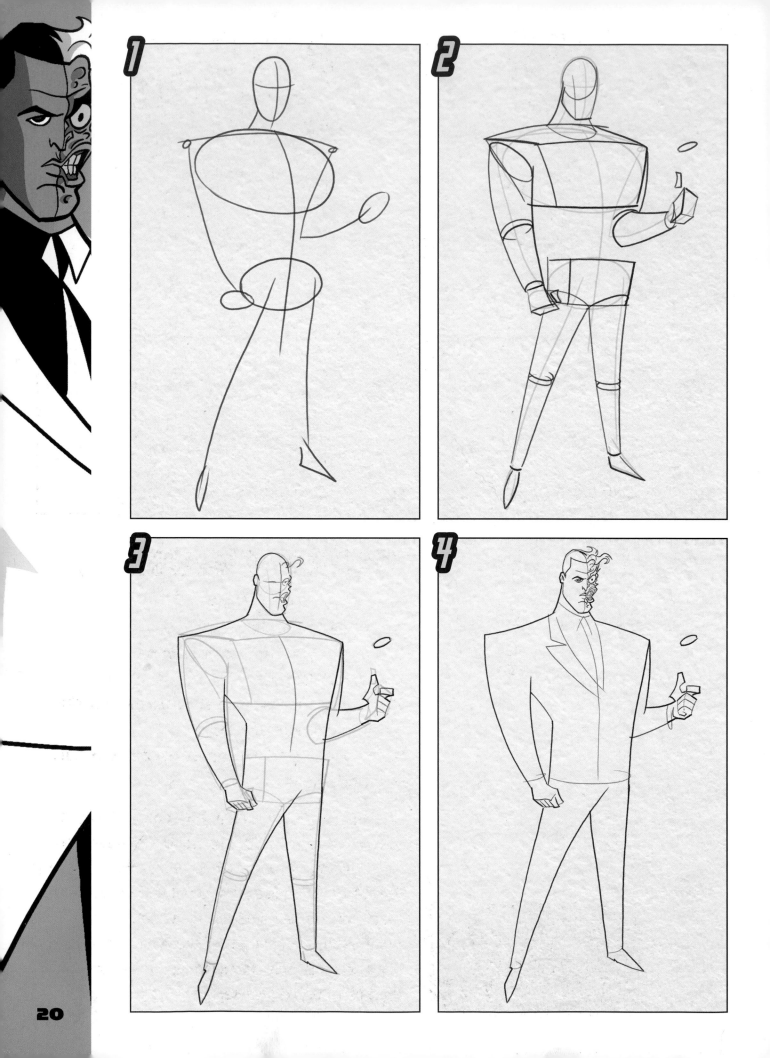

5

TWO-FACE

Real Name: Harvey Dent
Home Base: Gotham City
Occupation: professional criminal
Enemy of: Batman
Abilities: above-average strength and fighting skills, expert marksmanship
Equipment: special two-headed coin to make most decisions

Background: Harvey Dent was once the best lawyer in Gotham City. He worked tirelessly to send the city's most dangerous criminals to jail. But when an explosion scarred half of his face and body, Harvey's darker side took control. He became the criminal Two-Face. Now he tries to run the same criminal world he once fought so hard to bring to justice.

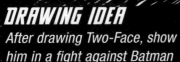

DRAWING IDEA
After drawing Two-Face, show him in a fight against Batman after robbing an armoured car.

21

THE PENGUIN

Real Name: Oswald Cobblepot

Home Base: Gotham City

Occupation: professional criminal

Enemy of: Batman

Abilities: genius intellect, numerous criminal connections

Equipment: trick umbrellas

Background: Oswald Cobblepot's waddling walk and beakish nose earned him the nickname of the Penguin. He is almost always protected by several hired thugs. The Penguin also owns a number of special umbrellas that hide a variety of deadly weapons. Among these are a machine gun, a flame-thrower, a sword, small blades and poisonous gas.

DRAWING IDEA
Next try drawing the Penguin using one of his special umbrella weapons to escape from Batman!

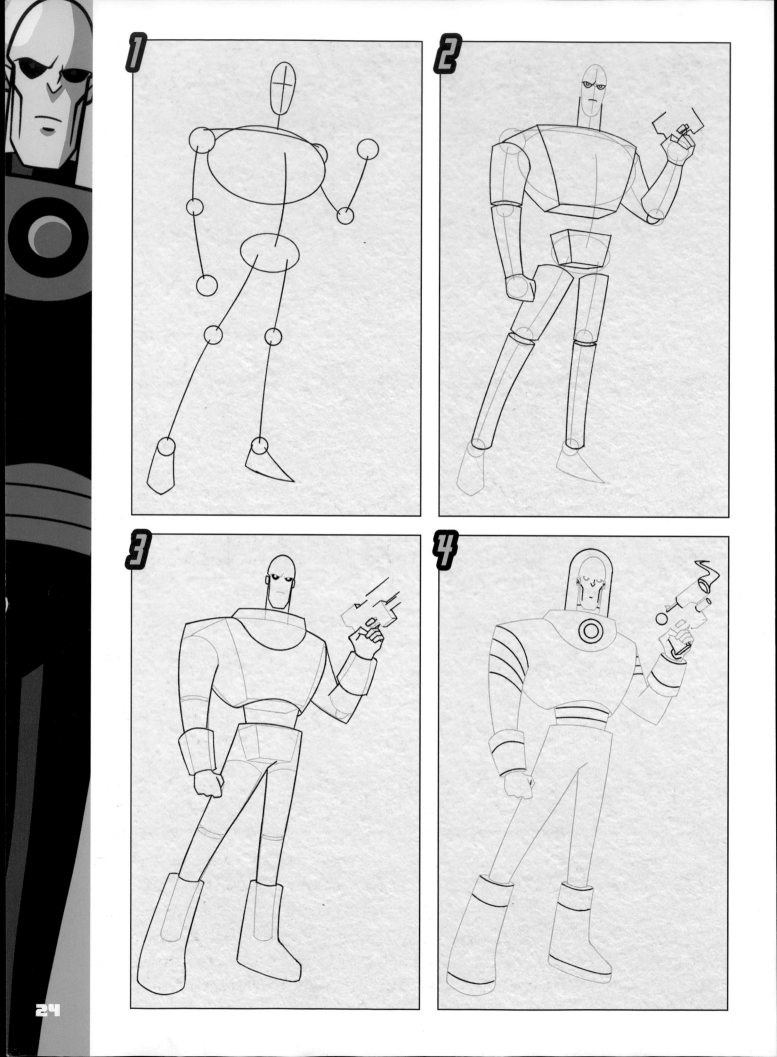

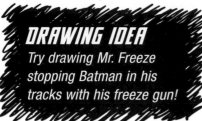
5

MR. FREEZE

Real Name: Dr. Victor Fries

Home Base: Gotham City

Occupation: scientist, professional criminal

Enemy of: Batman

Abilities: enhanced strength, genius intellect

Equipment: cryo-suit, freeze gun

Background: One day, scientist Victor Fries was accidentally soaked with chemicals in his lab. The accident changed his body so that he could live only at sub-zero temperatures. To survive, Victor built a special suit that keeps his body cold and gives him superhuman strength. To get the diamonds needed to power his suit, Victor turned to a life of crime. Calling himself Mr. Freeze, he uses a special freeze gun to aid him in his criminal activities.

THE RIDDLER

Real Name: Edward Nygma

Home Base: Gotham City

Occupation: professional criminal

Enemy of: Batman

Abilities: genius intellect

Equipment: question-mark cane containing hidden weapons and gadgets

Background: Edward Nygma loved riddles and puzzles as a boy. When he grew up he invented a popular video game called *Riddle of the Minotaur*. The game sold millions of copies, but Nygma never received a penny for his work. To get his revenge, he became the genius criminal the Riddler. He enjoys leaving cryptic clues to his crimes. Only Batman can solve the Riddler's puzzling crimes and put a stop to his wicked plans.

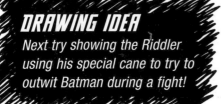

DRAWING IDEA
Next try showing the Riddler using his special cane to try to outwit Batman during a fight!

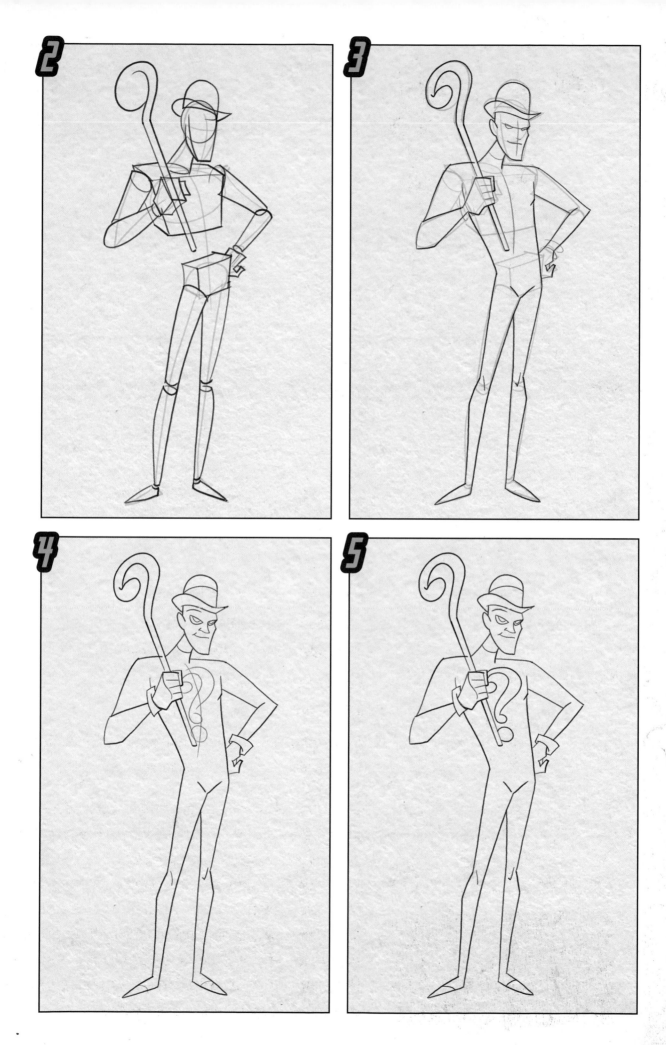

STOPPING THE JOKER

The Joker loves being Batman's arch-enemy. He's always hoping to get the better of the Dark Knight. The Joker enjoys designing weapons with a comical look to hide their true danger. For example, a huge bomb filled with deadly Joker Venom might look like a big party toy. But Batman is very familiar with how the Clown Prince of Crime thinks. He's always ready to swoop into action and put a stop to the Joker's plans before innocent people get hurt.

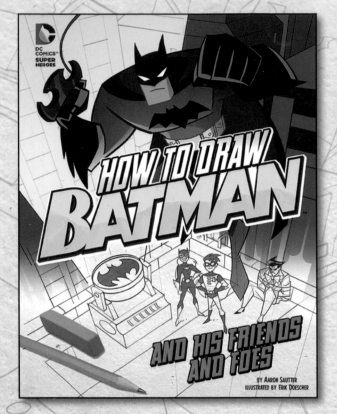

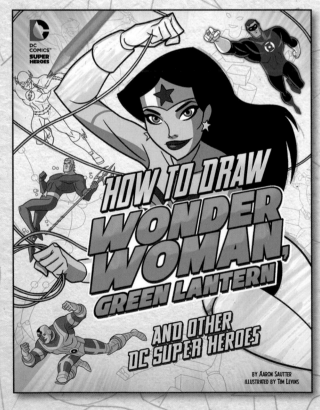